Love
Too
Much

I0624697

Love
Too
Much

poems

Charles Thomas

Copyright © 2024 Charles Thomas.

All rights reserved. No part of this publication may be reproduced, distributed, or transmitted in any form or by any means, including photocopying, recording, or other electronic or mechanical methods, without the prior written permission of the publisher, except in the case of brief quotations embodied in critical reviews and certain other noncommercial uses permitted by copyright law.

Cover and interior visual art by Jessica Saterstrom Eichman
jessicaeichman.com

ISBN: 978-1-95386584-7 (Paperback)
ISBN: 978-1-95386585-4 (eBook)

Library of Congress Control Number: 2024921349

Self published via Books Fluent
New Orleans, LA

For my mom and dad

who created breathing room for me
to dream and imagine when i was young
and who loved, thought, and felt deeply

Note: "Breathing room" is a term President Biden quoted from his father.

Contents

6

Preface

"It's later than it's ever been," so i want to live and love now, with both patience and action. The quote is from my dad. I'll address this living and loving in three contexts: community, personal, and family/nature.

As you read or listen, in addition to enjoying the wondrous visual art, please consider imagining a view of nature, birdsong, music, or rhythmic feel.

Love
Too
Much

Love Embodied in This Flame

As we light this chalice, we call to mind the fact that light is not inherently good. Yes, light contributes to life; yet light can burn and light can kill.

Just as light, white, and day do not represent good, neither do dark, black, and night represent bad. The imagery we choose makes a difference and may perpetuate stereotypes or negate stereotypes.

May love, as embodied in this flame and in ourselves, guide us.

Note: The purpose of this flame is not to dispel darkness. Love, as embodied in this flame, exists in the metaphorical heart of us, the actual heart and brain of us existing in darkness, within our bodies.

5

In Love

Rooting ourselves in love
      as the source of all we are

Let us love

Acknowledging every person and all of nature
      as unique, important, and wanted

Let us love

Learning that we are not whole
      until all beings are whole

Let us love

Sharing and relating with one another
      as each feels comfortable

Let us love

Working to be anti-racist
      and opposing every oppression

Let us love

Drawing nearer to Beloved Community
        on this our one planet

Let us love

Where Love Lives

The heart, the metaphorical center of emotion,
the metaphorical source of love, of care
—THE AUTHOR

If we could travel
into our physical hearts,
into our brains,
we would find darkness,
biophotons being too faint —
unless we activated
the lights on our phones. :-)

This darkness is where love
lives. This darkness
is where love begins the journey
outward to others, inside
to ourselves. It's where love
arrives when others send and give
love to us.

In this darkness, in this network
of weak electrical signals, love
grows, love soars like a nightjar,
love does what love does.

Together

Hoping to hide for a couple of hours
away from the burning light
of injustice where other
is other, instead of another,
we gather in the cool, refreshing dark
of community. In this place,
in this moment, other is not
other, but another the same as
yet different from, with identities
honored, respected, where in despair,
hurt, wrong, we are held, at this moment
along the zig-zagging route toward
reproductive freedom, the Equal Rights
Amendment, anti-racist racial justice,
BIPOC and LGBTQ+ rights to live in safety
and freedom, disability justice,
economic justice, environmental justice,
no more than 1.5 by 2030 justice,
we as wildflowers growing
at this service plaza along the turnpike,
extending roots, roots communicating
as flowers bloom. I want to be an ally
with those who are doing this work,
with those who have done this work for years,
with those who have died doing this work.
What will i do?
What will you do?
What will we do
together?

Worthship

Words of worth
rebound, resound,
walls cannot hold
the melody, the song
igniting fires, hearts
in motion, emotion
not alone, evolving
into revolution,
into action
for each one in the world
feeling alone,
unknown, reaching
to the root,
the radical source
Love.

Note: This poem was inspired by the sermons and homilies of the Rev. Catie Scudera and the Rev. Jenna Crawford, both at the time being part of the ministry team at First Parish in Needham, Unitarian Universalist.

The Eight Principles: An Impression

1
Each one wanted
Each one needed
Each one remembered
Each one loved

2
A hand reaching
to grasp another
even if on different paths

3
A hug, a smile
a sharing of thoughts
between us

4
A testing of ideas and actions
throughout our whole lives

5
Sharing our socially responsible views
even when another direction is determined

6
No more cries of hunger
No more cries of war
Only cries of joy

7
Blue Whales diving

Snowy Owls taking flight
You and i living
in concert with all

8
Learning and growing
Tearing down structures of discrimination and violence
Building a home for just and loving relationships

Note: Many Unitarian Universalist congregations have adopted the 8th Principle: "Journeying toward spiritual wholeness by working to build a diverse multicultural Beloved Community by our actions that accountably dismantle racism and other oppressions in ourselves and our institutions." As of this writing, the Unitarian Universalist Association has adopted a new statement of values and covenant based on the following: "Love is the power that holds us together and is at the center of our shared values."

Exquisite

exquisite exquisite exquisite
perfect exquisite
you perfect
she perfect
they exquisite perfect
black exquisite
ki he black perfect
night exquisite
you e perfect exquisite
rain exquisite
perfect black
you ki exquisite perfect
darkness exquisite
perfect ki e
perfect she exquisite
darkness ze exquisite perfect
they e exquisite
perfect perfect perfect
rain perfect
night ze they perfect
rain night he exquisite
darkness she ze exquisite
exquisite you
perfect perfect

Trauma warning: this poem references horrific events.

Us

Is theology possible
> after
the Middle Passage
> after
the auction block
> after
pogroms
> after
Gnadenhütten
> after
the Shoah
> after
infants
> thrown
> > in the air
> as targets
> > for weapons?

Or is theology possible
> only
> after
such horrors?

> A theology resembling

Altizer's Total Presence

> a Total Presence

which is a Total Absence

      which is a Total Presence

of us?

Note: Gnadenhütten refers to the massacre of 96 members of the Lenape people in 1782. Compare the late Thomas J. J. Altizer's concept of Total Presence, which is also the title of one of his books.

Trauma warning: this poem also references horrific events.

In God We Trust

Are you zoning out
already? I would be too
if i were talking about that god
who, some say, controls everything or
sometimes does and sometimes doesn't,
depending on the idea of someone
whose house does not lie 2x4 on 2x4,
nails poised to pierce feet,
whose loved ones do not lie, awaiting
slamming doors of hearse
upon hearse, curse upon curse, and
by the way, no karma
here, there, anywhere,
that god who tries to control you,
who tells you what to do, what not to do,
that god who allowed enslavement
to happen, who allowed genocides
to happen, attempted genocides
to happen, and still does.
No, i'm not speaking of that
idea of a god. I'm speaking metaphorically
of God embodied, your *self*, my *self*,
our *selves*, a community
making our best attempt not
to repeat such horrific events
and to remedy their systemic results.
I think i'll trust in this God
who is you and me and seekers of justice

and equity throughout history
who have lived, died, been killed
for their ideals, which have not yet
been realized. Do you agree with me,
that in this God we trust?

Note: As suggested by someone in a Unitarian Universalist study group, our own thoughtful and creative selves may be considered as metaphorical gods.

Trauma warning: this poem references blood.

Again

Concrete reeks
of iron, left-behind
of hemoglobin, after
what? After love
brought love into
being, body cushioned,
fashion-du-jour,
cyclists stop
their pedaling,
witnesses to themselves,
their beloveds, Beloved
Community far from
capitalist culture,
pedals become petals
of flowers.
Begin
again.

Note: According to thekingcenter.org the term *Beloved Community* was popular-
ized by Rev. Dr. Martin Luther King, Jr., and likely first used by Dr. Josiah Royce.

Of Bread

Are loaves uneaten
called leaves? Left roaming
or not as leaves on trees
roam or not?

What season is it, the season
to put up or take down
a tent, or are we on the way,
tents packed away in our gear,
searching the trail for berries or
reaching into backpacks
for energy bars as the meters
increase, or decrease,
or is it more than one
season, more than one reason,
all at the same time?

Planet Water Bead

The round
Zion of the water bead
my fellow Thomas wrote, of no
specific relation as far as i know yet
as surely a cousin to me as are you who
are reading this on a bright night or a dark
day, by candle, oil, battery-powered or electric
light, cousins all, living within a water-permeated
atmosphere, our Planet Water Bead not what it
used to be before captains of industry un-
furled their banners of unholy rule, and
our Body Water Beads, full of water-
bearing cells, seeking clean
water, which is often
difficult to find.

The round Zion of the water bead — from a poem by Dylan Thomas

Day

greets us

            like rising fawns

kissing

     dew-clothed

               meadows

nudging up

        against

              bodies

tired

sore

     calling us

           to write

the unwritten

        live

the unlived

love

the unloved.

Poetry of the Future

Poets, some of whom are known to be
brooding, cantankerous, withdrawing,
overdrawing folk, may still count
some of these among their number,
yet the future being more positive
will contain less and less to be mournful
and solemn about. Joy will replace
much of the sorrow. Writing for writing's
sake will replace much of the need
to lament. And yes, there will still be
poetry praising the beloved's lips and
heart and various parts, yet also poetry
praising every body, all ways of being.

No more dark/light, night/day, black/white
negative metaphors. No more *darkest hour*
imagery for bad or difficult things. No more
describing ice on roads as *black ice*. Give me
night, give me dark, so we can be in the black,
profiting from the absence of the white market
in racism.

This poetry of the future may produce
fewer tears, or it may produce more —
tears of happiness rather than sadness.

You know poets only declare the truth —
with a small *t* — as truth seems to them.
So comprehend ye, all the world,
this evangel of poetry shall come to pass

in the year
        2024

You understand that poets of the future
are always optimistic, always
wanting all to feel loved and be loved.

But actually, the future doesn't exist,
does it? Today is the seed of the hoped-for,
longed-for future world. Let's plant the seed,
which grows in the beautiful dark.

Note: I am grateful to the Rev. Catie Scudera — after i wrote this poem — for calling attention to W.E.B. DuBois's metaphor of today being the "seed time" for the future.

Receiving Rain

Grounded seed pods
brown, bountiful
receiving rain
beneath evergreen
leaves like eaves
hiding puddles of dogs
badgering you and me
to life when life
seems far away
but isn't,
it's here, it's
now, do you sense
the sweet scent?

Most

most.
si tsael si
like roots
e   v   o   L

10   12   3

Risk It

In the name of love
Risk it

Don't let the moment pass
Risk it

You may hurt if you do
Risk it

You will hurt if you don't
Risk it

Make real what you feel
Risk it

No regrets
Risk it

For justice
    For equity
        For equality
            For climate
                For Earth

For you
    For me
        For us
            For relationship
                For all

For love

Risk it

Lab Time

Don't forget love.

> *It's too sentimental.*
> *It's too mushy.*
> *You can't define it.*
> *You can't measure it.*

I have ki in me.

Do you have ki in you?

I think you do.

Let's experiment.

Note: The pronoun *ki* is used for living things other than humans. Isn't love alive?

Growing

Relationships can be complicated.
They don't always begin
that way. Isn't it simply
that like — the quiet initiator
of the possibility of love
like no other — leads to communication,
to conversation, to words
and actions taking root, going
deeper, wider, permeating
the soil of your life and mine,
of your experience and mine,
this little seed of some kind
of love, growing into the most
beautiful, delicate flower?

Free

Violet, free leaves
running to the sun
and back, seething down
meadows unowned,
unknown to the we
unborn, they sing
songs of longing
to trees tall as a ball
bounces, not once,
not an ounce of prevention
on the road
turning the tide
around for twice.

Present

And then
after books, after
apps, after picturing
corners of their mouth,
their laugh, after
all these non-invasive
ways of trying to reach
the interior of their heart,
their mind, they allowed
the moment to breathe,
they allowed the moment
to consume them
with joy for now

for the present
of their presence.

The Start

Fingers, focus,
the line connecting

you, me, us,
the start recedes

with care, concern
increasing, creasing

faces into smiles,
the race to now,

for now,
is not a race,

it's a place
touching

between us,
among us.

Today

I don't want to know
what forever feels like.

[Forever:
an unattainable point in time]

I want to know
what today feels like

[Today:
a time period that may be
repeated, with each day
filled with new joy]

with you.

Synonym

I could say your name, i could
fingerspell your name,
and if i could draw your smile
everyone who knows you would know
you're a synonym for love.

Yeah, this is a love poem alright,
there's no way over it. Maybe
being so direct is not what anyone
wants. Maybe being so direct
is just fine. Maybe being
so direct is my natural
inclination when a synonym
for love is so easy to understand.

Maybe a poem like this
doesn't belong in a collection.

Maybe a poem like this
is the only poem
that does.

(T)here

Here i am

There you are

Perhaps our shadows
touched

Touch
      to contact physically

Touch
      to connect emotionally

You touched
        my heart

Did i
      yours?

There i am

Here you are

A Non-GMO Love Letter on a Beautiful Day — Yes, a Dark and Rainy One

Non-binary bicycles
   buried beneath a surfeit
of surf, and you say
   sure, there has to be
a better way of weighing
   facts, figures,
your life on paper
   provided by trees —
your kin, my kin,
   kin to pineapples and
pines and apples,
   even the GMO kind?
My heart is with you
   and i want to dive
deeper and deeper.

In Motion

Gravity does not exist.
You may have learned otherwise.
Stars and planets and galaxies
are not attracted
by some mysterious force.
They and we roll downhill
in the stretching of space,
space and time part of the same
continuum. Does this explain
why, when you and i —
body and body — occupy
similar time and space,
we fall toward
each other?

Space-Time Between

You
1
2
3
4
5
line 6
10
7
9
11
8
13
12
line 14
line 15
17
16
line 18

22
21
19
20
line 23
line 24
line 25
line 26

29
31
28
30
27
Me

Limits

Limited is good,
don't you agree?
A free charge for your EV
limited to one hour — better
than only 30 minutes,
isn't it? Speed limits
to try to keep drivers, passengers,
pedestrians, cyclists, motorcyclists
safe — limited speeds are good.
That thing, that living
thing called love, even love
is good limited, at least
with some people. Maybe with
others you would rather have
unconditional, indescribable,
never-stopping, never-finishing,
can't-ever-get-enough,
unlimited love,
yet limited is still good,
isn't it?

Waiting

Waiting for leaves
to emerge, for fires
to burn

higher than they do now,
or maybe not higher,
maybe freer, maybe less

encumbered by wind and
rain, yet rain does
help things grow,

doesn't it? And wind
brings things unexpected,
and unexpected can be good,

can't it? Like the leap
in the heart of me
that i didn't know i was

missing. Like your words
that i didn't know
i was waiting for.

Difficult

It's the most difficult kind for me —
maybe not for you. Maybe it's easy
for you to let go of someone. For me,
letting-go love is much more difficult
than never-letting-go love. It's like
the difference between not falling
on ice, and falling on ice, at least it is
for me, unaccustomed to lacing on skates,
then trying my hardest not to fall,
not to break an arm or leg or wrist.
Oh, how i want to fall
over and over again in the same place,
never having to skate away.

Signs

Is there a sign, a signal
before leaves turn
kaleidoscopic, before
sunrise sings songs
never heard, never
felt? Or is art,
symphony the only
sign we get
when uniqueness
arrives unannounced
and oh, so welcome?
Is there a sign
before nature returns
to its previously wonderful
self, which now seems
so lacking?

Perfect

There is never
a time perfect
for it. What
is it, you say?
Oh, it could be
anything, say
telling someone
what they need
to know, what
you need to say,
what they could only
guess and turn
over and over
in their mind
with eyes closed
lying in bed until
sleep arrives. Did
i say *never*? I meant
always, always a time
perfect for saying
you bring me joy.

Create Now

This moment, alone
or shared between us,

this moment we make,
the only moment we have
to make, the moment before
something scheduled,
the moment after
something occurred.

Create life.
Create now, the only
now that is.

6

Part

You are part of Me
I am part of You

You are not Me
I am not You

Your life makes You
My life makes Me

Life does not make Truth

Note: I finished writing this poem in February 2020, just less than two years before i heard a Unitarian Universalist minister read Thich Nhat Hanh's lovely poem "Interrelationship." I like Thich Nhat Hanh's poem much better than mine. I believe both are true.

Capella

for my mom

When the waxing crescent
    continues the day

When the first quarter moon
        divides blue
           in half

When the waxing gibbous
               grows
   changes

When the full moon through the trees
     calls mockingbirds
        to sing the night

When the waning gibbous
    lights a path for fireflies
       to find their beds

When i'm always surprised
          by the third quarter moon
    in the morning

When i almost always miss
    the waning crescent
       a slice of sun up early

When Capella shines
   low in the northeast

Same as Five Months Ago

for my mom

a chickadee picks up a seed
flies to the cover of the spruce

a robin rushes through the grass
stops and looks and listens

a goldfinch perches and drinks water
whistles what sounds like a question

same as five months ago
when she smiled

while watching with me

It Must Have Been

It must have been those long walks down country lanes,
  daisies and black-eyed Susans separating dirt path from farmland,
your small hand reaching up and held in your mother's loving grip
  like a flower just picked. Every now and then

she let you run ahead to throw a clump of soil
  back into the field from which it came,
where a family's livelihood lay hidden,
  cotton and tobacco crops depending on

the right amount of rain at just the right time.
  Sometimes she let you walk barefoot,
usually nothing dangerous out there to step on,
  broken glass on concrete miles and a world away.

At times she would lift you safely across
  a normally dry creek bed swollen with water flowing
from the wet-weather spring. I wonder what
  she talked to you about during those once or more

weekly trips. Did she tell you that hard work
  and keeping your word were always most important,
even if they didn't pay? Did she say
  that hard times would come and like Yosef in Egypt

you would have to plan ahead? Whatever it was,
  she must have gotten through.
Maybe she sang songs of joy
  along with songs of sadness,

66   LOVE TOO MUCH

teaching you to love life and yet beware.
    Anyway, that must have been it,
those long walks
    down country lanes.

On Observing Light Just Arrived from Aldebaran

Crackling cold tonight, coldest
since '81's deadfall snow,
silvery ice wrapping every
branch, every twig tight.

Moon reflects and stars shine,
but not here in this house
empty of smiles,
of laughter.

The fire of your presence remains
despite our lack — coffee
not as strong, peppermints
not as sweet,

green-plaid fedora
unmoved, red-cedar aroma
emanating still.

Baking

Books and books baking
lakes full of linguini
wrapped in ribbons of wood
shaped by hands
directed, dictated
only by love, a love
of home and own,
not needing moving
place to purple
place, a silence

no one knows

no applause
defining parables
of freedom

Leaves

I don't like it,
leaves changing colors
in the fall before
they fall. I know falling
can be good. I've felt it.
I've known it. Leaves changing
colors is a process of nature,
be at one with it, it's been said.
It's a fact, yet i don't have to like it,
and i don't even
have to accept it.

My grandpa at 28,
lungs filling and falling
for the last time. This is a fact.
I don't like it. I don't accept it.
This was not something
coming toward us from the future
while we were meditating. We
move into the future, living
each moment.

        I would love
leaves changing colors,
if i were experiencing them
with someone who loves
experiencing them, with someone
i love.

helios

day dawning
   across the water

promising good
   to those who

from highest hill
   to lowest valley

from easy chairs
   to beds of pain

view its advent
   bathed in beauty

and wonder if
   it's only a show

zoe

light sent

from far

above

the forest

canopy

coursing

through a maze

of vines

of leaves

of twigs

falling softly

upon petals

of a delicate flower

called Spring Beauty

enabling

what we know

as life

anemos

foliage

falling

floating

down

blown by force

unseen

branches bare

alone

preparing for

new life

Reach

The force required,
never enough
to reach Bermuda,
leaps and keeps
left lying
around and down
to street level,
the beveled edge
a synthesis
of icicles frozen,
thawing, cycling
forward
to now.

Like

Like a rainbow
running away from you

Like a mountain you could touch
a hundred kilometers in the distance

Like 30 degrees Celsius
when it's 30 degrees Fahrenheit

Like the excitement of caf
when you drink decaf

Like stopping global warming
and temps keep rising

Later Than It's Ever Been

for my dad

Are you running late? I thought
i was. Late — after the appointed
time, after the time when registration

for the event i wanted to attend
is closed, when the connection
i wanted to make may no longer

be possible. I thought i was running
late, but actually i was early —
there before the special event,

there before someone was ready.
In the sense i'm speaking of, i can't control
whether i'm early or late. So really,

i guess i'm right on time, even though
it's later than it's ever been.

Maybe i should try to make today special.

Note: My dad used to say, "It's later than it's ever been."

Can't Be Done

There's a saying,
you can love
too much.
Is it true? I say
love is weak.
At least the kind of love
i'm talking about
is weak. And i say
this is the only true
love. Other loves
are loves in name only.
The kind of love i'm
talking about holds on
when meeting a reciprocal
love. This real love releases
when it's necessary
to release. This kind of love
allows time
                       allows space.
This kind of love is strong
in being weak. And yes,
i am trying to repeat *love*
as many times as possible.
How many times
have i said *love*?
Not enough times
in my life, neither telling
nor showing.
So go ahead,
try to love too much.

It can't be done.

Note: I don't intend to express that i practice well this kind of love; i am still learn-ing. And isn't there a continuum of love, from loving visual art, poetry, music, and all kinds of art, to loving someone who actually is irreplaceable — in contrast to Beyoncé's song? :-) At various places along this continuum of love, lie each of the loves in your life, in my life.

Afterword

While in the beginning stage of planning to self-publish a book of poems, i was very happy to get to know someone better who besides being interested in poetry is also a photographer and visual artist, among other things. I asked if she would be interested in providing the cover art for my planned book. She suggested the added possibility of illustrating some or all of the poems, and i immediately loved the idea. Although she is not the person who ultimately created the art that appears on the cover and at the beginning of each section of this book, i proceeded with her consent and want to thank her for her wonderful idea.

I added the trauma warnings to the chalice lighting words and to specific poems in this collection after the chalice lighting words were declined by *WorshipWeb*.

The lowercase letter *i*'s throughout are not typos :-)

Acknowledgments

Editors of the following publications liked these poems well enough to publish versions of them:

Friends Journal: "It Must Have Been"
Remington Review: "Capella," "On Observing Light Just Arrived from Aldebaran"
WorshipWeb of the Unitarian Universalist Association: "In Love," "Worthship"

Thank you to editors of other publications who published other poems of mine.

Thank you to my parents for their love. Thank you to my mom for reading to me when i was young, and for her example of love. Half of me is half of my mom. I mentioned breathing room on the dedication page; i want to note that many people work as much as my parents did, yet are unable to create any breathing room because of racism, prejudice, or other circumstances. I realize how privileged i have been.

Thank you to someone who was special to me for her idea of combining visual art with poetry.

I am grateful to my aunt Betty, who talked with my mom once a week and has continued talking with me once a week.

I am grateful to my aunt Jane for our conversations.

I am grateful to Rev. Catie for sharing her words of love and care via sermons.

I am grateful to Nora and to Helen for listening, accepting, and encouraging — without which i would not have had the confidence to begin sharing my words at open mics.

Thank you to open mic listeners online and in-person; and to Kory, Amie, and Kara for creating community among writers.

Thank you to all who have shared time and thoughts with me.

Thank you to Jessica Saterstrom Eichman for agreeing to create the visual art for this collection.

Thank you to Hannah, Jenn, Marisa, and others for your expertise in helping to make this book a reality and in helping to let the world know about it.

Almost all, if not all, of this poetry was written on the occupied territory of the S'atsoyaha, the Shawandasse, and the Tsalaguwetiyi peoples. Some of my ancestors held people of African ancestry in slavery.

About the Author

Charles Thomas writes for the joy of expressing his feelings and ideas. Twenty poems of his have been accepted and published by various print and online publications. Many more poems — plus chapbook and longer manuscripts — have been declined. He decided to self-publish this collection in order to share some kind of joy and some kind of feeling with readers and listeners. Not having an MFA in poetry, he wants to encourage a lack of fear in presenting your own creativity and imagination.

About the Visual Artist

Jessica Saterstrom Eichman is an artist who works and lives in Nashville, Tennessee. A native of Natchez, Mississippi, Jessica earned degrees in Art and French before living and working in Paris, France; Corvallis, Oregon; and Boston, Massachusetts. Jessica's paintings have been exhibited in the Huntsville Museum of Art, Nashville International Airport, and numerous private galleries, and have been featured in print and online. Her work can be found in public and private collections across the country and internationally, including the permanent public art collection in the Nashville Historic Metro Courthouse and Hermitage Park in Nashville.

For more, including an artistic statement, go to jessicaeichman.com

www.ingramcontent.com/pod-product-compliance
Lightning Source LLC
Chambersburg PA
CBHW051643120626
46551CB00015B/2192